Get
Out Go
Alone
Get
Away

Get Out Go Alone Get Away

Bill Haywood

atmosphere press

I want to thank my wife, Wahneta, for her essential assistance in
putting this collection together. Also, my daughter, Liz,
who created the graphic art displayed in the poetry book.
Finally, the staff at Atmosphere Press for their input and expertise
to make this book a reality.

ANYONE

Who loves to feel cool wind on their face
and beneath their feet, dry leaves cracking,
to watch cotton clouds across sky race
and wish to be on earth's trail tracking –
to kindle a remembrance, deja vu
and lift a smile while spirits renew.
With these forty poems I paint five seasons,
connecting you with creation's reasons.

- Bill

INTRODUCTION

There is a basic unity connecting annual and perennial plants, shrubs, and trees. They all rely upon the sun to produce energy necessary for their existence. In doing so, they evolved into communities that share the physical resources of the earth and the reception of essential light. That path of evolution included animals, fungi, and microbials, all which rely on plants for their energy. Human beings are part of that community.

Genuine impressions can be gained when consciously stepping away from everyday turmoil. In writing these poems, I wanted to provide images that would connect the reader to the simple peace and beauty of the natural world. These poems represent an awareness of how science, the arts, and spirituality are interwoven into our lives.

The hiking journeys in my poems are placed within five "seasons" of a year. It's a reminder that everything on earth, in our galaxy, and within our universe is subject to time. Every component of nature has a lifespan that ends – only to be reformed as renewal begins again. The cycle goes on forever.

CONTENTS

Autumn Afternoon

Autumn's Amity
Arcadia
Obsolete
Inscribed Stone
Artisans
Impulsive
Bustling Commune
Camaraderie
Contemplation

Indian Summer Twilight

Venerable Passage
Optimism
Carry in Thought
Ultimate Excursion
Trust

Winter's Repose

Nurturing
Sylvan Shrine
Simple Subsistence
Sole Encounter
Radiance
The Hiker's Prayer

SPRING MORNING

AWAKENING

Get out. Go alone. Get away.
Find nature's simple peace each day.
Avoid the artificial congestion.
Disappear from the trivial question.
Smell, taste, feel, see, and hear
what is true, beautiful, and near.

God's greatest revelations
made in places of isolation.
Siddhartha, the forest Buddha,
Jesus in the wilderness of Judah –
as God's son, humanity to save –
and Mohammed in Mt. Hira's cave.

Forest, prairie, marsh, and sea,
earth, moon, sun, and galaxy.
Open your senses to what's real
in which land, water, and sky reveal.
Just one God, just one soul –
let tranquility be your goal.

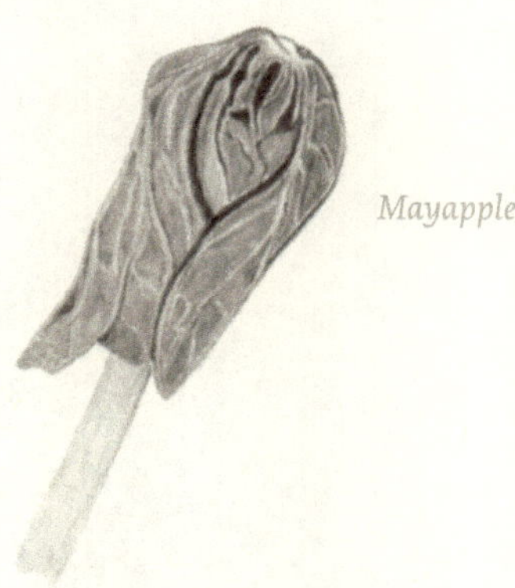

Mayapple

FIRST CREATION

Our grand, old gravity!
Without its subtle pull
wonder what we would be?
Just dark and very dull.

Fading cosmological phantoms
at light speed outward traveling –
as electromagnetic quantum
in a universe unraveling.

No earth and no sun,
only bits of obscurity.
Big Bang and then done
without substantiality.
But if no gravity...
no Big Bang ideality!

CELESTIAL GENESIS

A microscopic bubble of compressed energy,
mass and energy, ten-billion-degree synergy.
Initiating space, at light speed expanding
to cause hydrogen and helium matter banding.
Gravity's pull, the first crucibles consolidate,
the other ninety atoms supernova create.
Star dust into the expanding void blowing
so, our sun and planet, their form come glowing.

On a clear, rural, moonless night,
multitudes of stars the only light.
The galaxy displayed in marvelous presentation,
a perfect view of the magnificent creation.
Years in billions of constructed evolution,
continuously changing, a renewing revolution.
The heavens vast light years in radius,
what wonders out there do await us.

Beyond here what is mankind's place
in eternity's infinite, universal space?
Does one sun, one earth, one presence suffice,
with endless time and such enormity, what is one life?
Standing here alone, quietly looking up,
what significance could possibly be my cup?
What wisdom gained when released from corporal ties –
within the essence of God, the secret lies.

GOODBYE TIME

The chains of Master Time are broken,
no longer his command be spoken.
Served his wishes throughout my prime,
now "goodbye" to mean Master Time.
Not waiting for tomorrow's sun
or counting hours till job is done.
Going back to where it began,
back when freely my spirit ran.

Nature's beauty a lush laboratory
and time no burden as a child,
out of mind when exploring wild.
All trails twist a rich depository,
surprise flowed with each new territory.

Time brought responsibility
and drug that harness over me.
Wonder dissolved under the whip,
crushed all pleasant plans with that grip.
Surprise sunk to others' expectations,
dreams diverted to dim speculations.

Have now put that behind me,
never more to be time's slave,
the future here is mine to save.
Now all work, by choice, is free,
this day's mine to breathe and be.

Will rekindle curiosity –
every bird in flight will stop to see.
Any colored stone beneath my feet,
stoop to inspect the sparkling treat.
Smell the wood's organic scent,
hear coyote's musical lament.
Watch water swirling in the creek,
enjoy the wind brushing my cheek.
Every sunrise a discovered treasure,
tonight's sunset a moment of pleasure.

FELLOW COMPANION

Early sun boldly streaming light,
full round, above horizon bright.
While walking along high hill's crown,
throws a spectral image down
on the long swale slope below –
it's my hiking companion, Shadow!

Distanced, stop, go or run;
sequenced, we move as one.
Bound fast, kindred to each other,
same origin, brother to brother.
Created by light of nuclear fusion,
we're both more than just illusion.

Gradually the solar elevation
draws us together, one compilation.
Shortening the spatial distance,
connecting our single existence.
Joined as one, feet touching feet,
starting the day now complete.

Regardless of wind, cold or heat,
all that strife lays in defeat,
futilely unable to out-compete
the radiant power that lets us meet.
So now until clouds darken the air,
we venture forth, adventures to share.

RENASCENT

The first sound of early spring
is to hear the cardinal sing.
Flashing its plumage scarlet red
from the branches just overhead.

Old snowdrift remnants with winter stain,
tinkling meltwater in rivulets drain.
Composting microbes, their industry lift
rich, organic odors as a thin mist.

Trillium and trout lily emerge from duff,
bloodroot wrapped, hepatica covered in fluff.
Soon to bring beauty after winter so cold,
the new buds renewing life from roots so old.

FLEETING PRESENCE

Tufted, puffy clouds of cumulus
floating, flowing in blue above us.
Imaginary phantoms, edges deforming
into elusive creatures briefly forming.
Southeast sailing in new season's air,
white balloons lead earth's spring fair.

Silky shadows chase sunlight from ground,
shade sprinting across without a sound.
Light in flight, retreating at equal pace,
then appearing behind, taking its place.
Tandem waves skimming soil's undulations
driven to reach final destinations.

Only the present of prime importance now,
yet, instantly gone as turf to the plow.
Fourth dimension of the universe –
can't be stopped or put in reverse.
The clouds as smoke, their presence so brief,
does time leave joy or does time leave grief?

On far knoll the township cemetery,
migrant souls rest without commentary.
Spirit's legacy, either light or dark,
in soil and dust, an extinguished spark.
Headstones flashing, shade to shine,
what rewards this race, our own design.

CONFIDENCE

Silence broken, enchanting and eerie,
strong, solid and bold, not weak or weary.
The call "Yip, Yip, Howooo," sings exultantly.
The crowning final note ebbs elegantly
as the howl echoes deep into the west
announcing from the hills' encircling crest:
"I am Coyote and I am here!"

VERNAL ABLUTION

As snow cover dissolved, it revealed
the soiled, tattered remnants
of a winter-weary land sealed.
Juncos, black caps, and tree sparrow
flitting under bushes to harrow
the hidden seeds of last fall.

Pleasant wind, stronger than weak,
whooshing past the ears,
caressing the face and cheek.
Whispering through tall white pines,
rustling the worn, brown grass lines,
new blades emerging green and fine.

Scaling the horizon, a dark wall
underlined by tan, crushed corn stubble,
troubled sky, a mural above all.
Big rainstorm to the ominous west,
a time to pause, retreat, and rest.
Far away deep thunder is rolling.

Honoring the powerful arrival,
birds vanish for shelter and survival,
the cordial breeze rushes to escape.
Advancing fingers now overhead,
light gives way to dark's murky tread.
The present obscure, with hope, we wait.

Scattered, fat raindrops heavily splash,
followed by the soaking deluge.
Lightening hidden within clouds' mash,
their searing slash the land sparing.
The hardwoods stand bare, not caring,
while the pine bend and whip in the wind.

The storm had no time to waste,
pushing on into the accepting east.
The cleansing clouds swirl with haste
leaving the air pure and thatch clean.
Birds, trees, and grasses reconvene,
a refreshing renewal, like spirit-revealing truth.

BENEFICENT

What makes the blossoms cling
to thin limbs of wild plum?
Poses quite a conundrum!
Freezing nights, winter not done,
weather can be ever so glum
here, in cold, early spring.

What make the blossoms cling
like a queen's graceful entrance?
White blooms in royal elegance,
each in symmetrical sequence,
airing their sweet fragrance
from branch sprays in a ring.

What makes the blossoms cling,
opening with April's half moonlight,
lasting until crescent gone from sight?
Oh! Of course – seems only right,
it's for honeybees' waking delight!
That's why the blossoms cling
so early in our spring.

SUMMER'S HIGH NOON

TRANSFORMATION

In elapsed time immemorial,
stromatolites and brachiopods,
corals and sponges primordial.
Beneath a warm Silurian sea,
a flourishing marine world plods.
Early life submerged, pristine and free.

Using calcium and carbon bound
to form a protective shell around
as nurtured within the limey sound.
Vast generations thrive and expire,
shells disintegrating or entombed,
sinking to press a bottom entire.

Buried shells, faultlessly molded,
hollow in the confining floor,
while a shrinking sea unfolded
a drying of the ancient bed.
For millennia, wet and dry,
the ocean surged and fled.

Each drying left precipitation
of silicon dioxide on the wall.
Coat by coat, perfect imitation
covering each thin crystal spread,
until filling the extinct fossil all
with sparkling clear molecules wed.

Age after age of relentless time,
the gem solidly confined.
Sea disappeared, as rose the lime,
glaciers on formations descended,
burying the interment with debris
before forests and prairies ascended.

Rain rivulets cut the plateau
and gashed into the limestone and clay.
Ravines exposed the soft stone below,
melting the enclosing cast away.
Brilliance was cleaned of carbonate bonds,
at last in sunlight the beauty lay.

From life-giving water and light,
the perfect shape of ancient delight,
before locked in death's deep, dark vent,
four hundred thirty million years spent.
Again, the water removed the night,
to yield this gemstone shining bright.

MINSTREL

No outline to show a face,
no color to allow inspection,
without bulk to fill a space,
too thin for light reflection.
No site to mark a birthplace –
seeks no profit from its conception.

Summer breeze blowing,
where has it been,
where is it going?
What has it seen,
what is it knowing?

Arrives without initiation,
gliding by without termination,
revealed only by agitation.
Puts leafy treetops dancing,
low herbs waving and prancing.
Floating butterflies go flittering,
smooth, glassy ponds set jittering.
Wafts the perfume of flowers,
at times, leads late afternoon showers.

This same air swept the glacier's face
and moved the loess into its place.
Brushed the big blue and Indian grass,
spread their fluffy seeds with each pass.
Fluttered the petals of the prairie flower,
blew the pollen so plants renew,
gave draft to the hawk's hovering view.

In spite of all the manmade changes,
tilled ground and river rearranges,
still here today, does yet appear
when the hot, humid days are here.

Starts in motion each sunny day new,
dries the heavy early morning dew,
softens the bite of afternoon heat
and does what it can to help us sleep.

Plies the plains with soft music.
Whispers lyrics by bright daylight,
hums lullabies by dark of night.
And so, it will until end of earth,
its soothing concert earns its worth.

NATURE'S COHESION

Upon the flowering continent
or in the bountiful blue sea
during any age of ancient earth
nothing in nature can compliment
the majestic, wonderful tree.

The trunk with ligneous strength
either short or clean with length
resilient against storm's fury.
Weathered, rough, curled bark ridges
blue-green lichens splotch the edges.

Cellulosic bole rising straight and stout
before arraying limbs go up and out
curving skyward to present the green.
Hundred-foot apex reaching so lofty
crown fifty feet from proxy to proxy.

Tufts of leaves the sun pleasing,
tenaciously attached, the wind teasing.
Radiant energy blending and cleaving
forming sugars for building the cell
of roots and helpful microbes as well.

Growing in communities the tree's intention,
feather, fur and fungi gain protection.
Amidst with shrubs and herbs, all accompanying,
soil, minerals, and water they are conserving.
The forest – earth's greatest gift for preserving.

SOLAR FLAMES

A small flickering orange glow
heating the dry limb bundle
from the tinder stuffed below.
Oxygen attacks each hot molecule,
breaks into ions the cellulose fuel.
Increasing the kinetic energy
by severing the hydrogen bond,
freeing carbon by magic wand.
Water vapor and CO_2 forming,
rising, smoky fumes the air warming.

The flames dance in buoyant jubilee
within the blazing, gassy stream
like frothy waves on a windy sea.
Eyes watch the cheery luminosity
drawn to the alluring curiosity.
Pulling, flaring, swaying, whipping,
radiant tongues from wood flipping.
Vibrant orange, yellow, and flicks of blue
stretching, sparking, yearning to be free
after decades confined within the tree.

But the wood and the flame are one,
obtaining the spirit of unity
solely from the power of the sun.
In cycles of life, green plants grow,
the friendly fire lets us know
from light they come, in light they go.
The limbs dissolve to mineral ash,
the coals give a final, firefly flash.
Fascinating chemistry drove the cremation
coloring this amazing transformation.

NOBILITY

Daring line of raptors ancestral
ruling between soil and sun.
Possessing the wind, the Kestrel –
nature's perfection, a noble one.

Bluish feathers adorn the wings,
painted bands beside the eyes.
A warning above earth it flings,
"Killi, killi, killi," the hunter cries.
On high pole or steep ledge narrow,
observing the sod for mouse or snake,
beware the careless sparrow,
swiftly striking, a meal to take.

Seen scanning the land from vantage height
or hovering above concealing grass,
the smallest falcon, with precise sight,
moving with summer as seasons pass.

Full life with one partner pairing
while traversing the central plateau,
every danger and success sharing
from Mexico to Canada's lingering snow.
Strength and beauty the hawks display
as over the rolling plain they fly.
Knight of the thermals, soaring by day,
freeborn sojourner of prairie sky.

SOOTHING DARKNESS

Into the bottomland forest night
walking under the full moon's might
shedding patches of yellow white
through waving openings at tree height.

Biscuit clouds spaced up high
scampering across soft-lit sky
casting figures of spooky lore
onto the lush herbal floor.

The south brisk breeze comes swirling,
tall cottonwoods – their leaves purling.
Swamp oaks, gnarly limbs in adoration
praising the night's cool restoration.

West Fork River's current laughing
as over sunken snags goes splashing.
Moon reflecting off the alluvial tea
wishing well the waters return to sea.

Many sounds only kin to the dark –
horned owl hoot and mother deer bark.
Small creatures rustle quick and furtive
bullfrog croaks loud and assertive.

Nocturnal wrap provides protection,
offers the time for calm collection.
Shaded shadows strip daylight's illusions
so thoughts reach reasonable conclusions.

HARMONIOUS BALANCE

In the still summer morning
after night's pleasant cooling
before the sun's daily warming.
Easy, slow, melodious cooing.
Season's vows they are renewing,
mourning dove, its mate wooing
from the mulberry above the slough.

Teardrop crystals of pure dew
condensed from the humid air,
glistening, shimmering, hanging new,
precariously from the leafy edges
of marsh herbs and tall sedges.
Some flash with reflection bright,
others spectrum-split into rainbow light.

Delicate, yellow, slipper flowers
as gondolas below Jewelweed leaves
open to pollinators just a few hours.
Throat speckled with red to infrared,
ensuring bumblebees are led
before the afternoon heat
wilts petals in temporary sleep.

Shining silver spider webs
stretched between dead plant stems
gently pulse as breath flows and ebbs.
Arrowhead leaves point to heaven,
arrayed in marsh fern's congregation
next to crowded cattail concentration.
The green, swelling as dough with leaven.

Fragrant scent of sweet clover
seeps down from meadow to hover
above the mysterious marsh affair.
Bank swallows gracefully sweep the air.
Helios brilliant this July morn.
Fading white moon in far west urging
sun back from Cancer to Capricorn.
Nature in balance, a calm merging.

QUIET ENLIGHTENMENT

Idle talk just a waste of breath,
frivolous chatter filling space of time.
What difference, between birth and death,
why discuss the daily, human crime?

Better to guide feet on rocky walk,
maybe catch sight of a sailing hawk.
Wash the mind free of small people's grime
and open senses to nature's rhyme.

Wait to save precious words for tonight,
thoughts always deeper without the light.
Body fatigued, sprawling near campfire,
now the hour for wisdom to inspire.

The misty Whisps of the Woods draw near,
faint Prairie Wind Spirits you can hear.
Night Sky Haloes descend fraternally,
all mingle amidst congenially.

With darting, fiery sparks they cheer beauty
forged without greed's gold, fame, or duty.
Paint hummingbirds and flowers where they dine,
songs of splashing rivers and swishing pine,
carve ancestral images in worn oak
and write God's thoughts, the deep depth to evoke.

MAJESTIC MESSENGER

Climb mighty thunderhead, climb,
rising to heights towering.
This is your eminent time,
turbulent heat powering
with warm air ascending,
cooling columns descending,
the tumbling clouds pillowing,
Cumulus congestus billowing.

Cast your bolts of lightning,
roll your deafening thunder,
tempestuous winds frightening,
split hot summer asunder.
Dispel the still, stagnant air,
force flitting songbirds to ground,
drive the red fox to its lair,
the land, astound with your sound.

Proclaim your powerful wrath,
great Lion of the Atmosphere.
Make the stubborn blind see your path
and those who won't listen, hear.
Leave earth in attentive awe.
Hand posterity a story
by imposing Pangea's law
with your brief burst of glory.

SENTINELS

Flight of zigzagging dragonflies
skimming, darting, guarding the skies.
Gleaning mosquitoes on the rise
in sight of their huge compound eyes.
No time to harvest gold pollen tips,
no interest in sweet nectar sips.
Feasting only on winged protein bits
buzzing into their aerial circuits.

Chasing, dodging, gleefully zipping
following my rambling path dipping
among the wetland herbs and grasses
by the tall, flowing prairie patches.

Two hundred million years sustaining,
all that time so busy restraining
clouds of the fiendish, blood-thirsty pest
which have raged, swarmed, and stung without rest.
Dragonflies are still near, keeping air clear
with dazzling aeronautics giving cheer.
We can only thank God that they are here!

AUTUMN AFTERNOON

AUTUMN'S AMITY

Showing first in trees' upper loft,
autumn appears so hushed and soft.
Yellow, golden, and scarlet tinting,
colors whisper what Libra's hinting.
Helping summer to finish the race
shifting gently to assume its place.

Quiet calls as dark passes twilight,
slowly cold settles deep in the night.
Barely arriving before night is through,
changes happen to the sultry dew.
On lush herbs forms a frosty fleece,
suggesting soon all growth will cease.

At dawn's first blush, warm light comes creeping,
satin crystals turn wet and weeping.
Fall not rushing to make the transition,
respecting summer's copious tradition.
Winter won't, to fair autumn, be so nice,
burying colors and smells with snowy ice.

Between now and impending white sleep,
applaud the free-sailing leaves piled deep.
As life's productive chlorophylls decline,
carotenoids and anthocyanins shine.
Turning fresh green to auburn coloration,
each day a new, beautiful elaboration.

ARCADIA

Just a little rocky crick
in the once rich prairie earth.
Draining the land on the quick,
ends a few miles from its birth.

So doing since the glacier's trip,
winding, curving in its course
like a busy herdsman's whip,
then dissolving in river's force.

Precious black loam narrowly sliced to show
what the grassy savanna did bequeath.
Then opening the glacial till below
to reveal the stones buried beneath.

Pebbles of quartz, rhyolite, and jasper
color the sharp bends in the swift stream.
Splashing, singing, gurgling, moving faster
as the flow zips the narrow seam.

Speeding between granite boulders
dug from the ancient base of Lake Superior,
swirling back, cutting the shoulders
before entry into a wooded interior.

Spreading into a placid pool
shaded by two gnarly old willows –
small spot where stream can clear and cool
ringed by wild herbs and grassy pillows.

A place to take a mental break
from civilization's fiery breeze.
Home of leopard frog and bull snake,
coned crawdad burrows in the muddy squeeze.

Meadowlark sings on milkweed,
minnows school in shadow water.
In here the spirit is freed –
worth saving for son and daughter.

A tiny piece of rare ecology
not yet crushed by Big Ag's heavy feet.
Still displaying nature's mythology
dating back to Eden's lush retreat.

This quiet and peaceful oasis,
refreshing as a good night's sleep,
where hate and strife have no basis,
most worthy treasure we can keep.

OBSOLETE

In the old black oak retreat,
midway across the limestone steep.
On a deer trail of trampled frass,
too narrow for either to pass.

Midday, no reason to meet,
we stopped surprised, head to feet.
Black rat snake advancing in slither
gave a look to make me wither.

Cautious, tense, ready to clear
"What are you doing here?"
we simultaneously exclaimed.
"I live here!" Obsoleta proclaimed.

The snake tasted my presence
with a quick flickering tongue.
Not liking the human essence,
distrusting us ever since young.

Although pleasant was my conversation
it bore no friendly manifestation.
The serpent's suspicions were maintained
and did not enjoy being detained.

"You are the intruding stain
within these woods where I reign,"
it assailed me with irritation.
I leaned to hear its enunciation...

Bolting quick over the mayapple leaf,
on top of the green, I, in disbelief.
Faster than a sparrow, snaking on air,
disappeared downhill, likely to its lair.

In a pensive mood, having meant no harm
while walking across the sterile grain farm.
Wondering about me and the confined snake,
two fading peculiars approaching our wake.

INSCRIBED STONE

Lush, green, dark forest stands large,
centurion trees the banner bearing.
With shrubs and herbs in their charge,
diverse community, light sharing.
Chlorophyll molecule the binding cloth –
prickly ash, bloodroot, and luna moth,
fox squirrel, nuthatch, and fungal broth.

Soil sliced and sloped by millennial rains,
erosion opens the path to earth's mystery.
Painted walls depicting losses and gains
by nature's power on the land's history.
Exploring the cool, shaded ravine,
viewing the many changes between
now and three hundred million years unseen.

Descending from fertile ground on top
through the till of grinding glacier's scene.
Down to the worn, sculptured bottom's stop
formed by Devonian seas pristine.
Earth's story in colored, perished pages,
ancient oceans, beaches, and plains in stages,
each era recorded in layers by ages.

For life ruling each environment,
their fossils affirm change, slowly fermenting,
making way for low-life's advancement,
wiping away royalty unrelenting.
None of the quenched species caused instability
by bleeding the land for profitability
and harming ocean's amending ability.

Five extinctions lay in geology
with a sixth occurring in our presence.
What lessons revealed to future archeology
about our flora and fauna's lost essence.
Not with ice, lava, or meteorite,
instead caused by human's reckless might,
that's raising earth's temp to lethal height.

Will the refreshing forest above face doom,
unable to change and survive our being?
To fade away as flower's dying bloom –
is there a prophesy on walls I'm seeing?
With wisdom we can stop the extermination
and promote nature's gracious manifestation.
If not, a stony film marks the dissipation.

ARTISANS

Precambrian cradle their humble story,
silently rising without oratory.
From tidewater's wash to renew life's glory,
sorting carbon from death's turmoil.

Fine mats of tiny chitinous threads,
by stitch, through wood, turf, and humus spreads.
Hidden from he who casually treads,
creating deep richness in soil.

Working beyond the radiant light,
never concerned if it's day or night.
Only stopped by frigid winter's might,
secretly, tirelessly, they toil.

Using pure chemistry and persistence,
having little physical assistance
to sustain their ascetic existence,
detritus their cheap, paltry spoil.

Magical the molecular dissolution
of organics to dusty resolution.
Guiding sparse minerals back to solution
for use by the verdant bloom.

Then the mysterious moment does arrive,
hyphae braids mycelium to surprise.
Stipe and pileus visible to the skies,
painting the phantom mushroom.

A mythical fairyland assimilation,
ephemeral in its manifestation.
With one purpose for the configuration,
spores swept away by wind's broom.

Devils Urn, Earth Star, and Lepiota,
Inky Cap, and Golden Pholiota,
Shaggy Mane, Scarlet Cup, and Amanita –
mystic masters of earth's tomb.

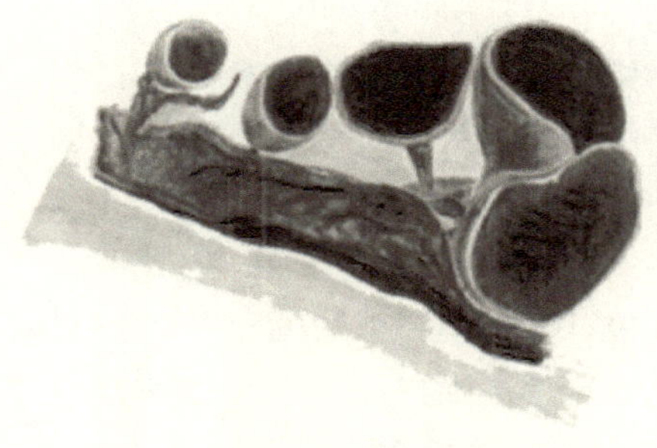

IMPULSIVE

Shadow rapidly skimming the ground
with a loud, tinkling, discordant sound.
Buoyant red wings congesting the sky,
elastic flock of thousands up high.
With lively energy they pirouette,
a choreographed cascade onto the set.
Curving beyond the weedy slough,
moving as one, sweeping on through.
Splitting, one half up remaining in flight,
gregarious rest on tall trees to light.
Raucous singing ever so bright and gay,
celebrating sunshine, relishing the day.

But wait, way up a hawk is sketched,
riding warm thermals, broad wings stretched.
Lazy drifting, watching the regale,
far above the playful birds' ballet.

Suddenly plunging, feathers and wings tucked tight,
bursting the formation into panic and fright.
Back into the heights ascending,
then once more swiftly descending.
Ripping through the cottonwood perches,
wings explode with hysterical lurches.
The red tail away into the sun –
did the mischief just to have some fun.

BUSTLING COMMUNE

Buzzing, bustling bumblebee,
endlessly searching to see
flowers needing pollen brushing.
Does the work for a small fee,
then back to hive goes rushing.
Underground comb in burrow nest,
at daylight's end, stops to rest.

Tenacity their true attribute,
foraging each day so resolute.
A black and yellow identity
but has construction inferiority.
With wings too small for body so plump,
lands on fresh blossoms with a bump.

Distaining animal superiority,
colony defense its priority.
Socially working, earning a living,
governed by royal authority.
Therein sharing harvest, freely giving
while tending waves of floral drapery,
lives a blissful life in the apiary.

Season ends with the purple aster,
the worker's days are short thereafter.
Queen holds the path to immortality
as bees disappear into the pasture.
She hibernates through winter's finality,
in green spring, renews the colony,
graced again with summer's harmony.

CAMARADERIE

Me and that best friend, dog,
not in a wayfaring rush.
Skirting broadside the wet bog
on a path through coralberry brush.
His focus is on a new scent,
nose just grazing the ground,
following where the coon went
while hunting the water round.

We are both peppered with seed pickers
hitchhiking for a free ride.
Spanish needles and beggar stickers
stuck to shirt and short-haired hide.
Along the wetland dredge,
now where is that curious dog?
Concealed by cattail edge,
distracted by a leaping frog.

Up onto the prairie tier,
wind blowing crisp and clear
across the grassy topography
under sky's blue-white choreography.
This wild beauty not from mountains high
nor does a crashing shoreline appear.
It's with flowing, floral fountains by
which one feels the majesty here.

Tallgrass sea a scene of motion
on the rolling lay of the land.
Cadence, set by wind's notion,
waving silver the bluestem stand.
Bobbing, flaxen Indian grass
streams down the moist swale.
Blazing star and goldenrod pass
summer's last colors to hail.

All connected, close affinity
between open vista and the past
where the nomadic identity
was upon the timeless land cast.
Paleo explorers, their spears
tipped with the fluted clovis point,
arrived here back ten thousand years,
the native people to anoint.

The dog from wolf they weaned and tamed
to form a firm fraternity
whose instincts to hunt still remained
sharing an ancient duality.
Unmuzzled by the restless breeze,
out here, that loyal dog runs free.
Freedom, no master must he please,
it's his choice to journey with me.

Following the canine's vocation,
methodically gaming forward and back.
Yet always knows my location,
included now as one of the pack.
Life-long friends always bond equally,
accepting each other's disparity,
while honest to self ethically –
it's the true meaning of liberty.

CONTEMPLATION

Out of the north below a canopy of gray,
effortless, no rebuttal, wind up at break of day.
A true taskmaster, with utmost efficiency,
morning spent dissolving the drab consistency.

Abrading up and up into heights ascending
until light to autumn's earth began descending.
The visibility was cold, clear, and bright,
a simple blue behind veils of wispy white.

Work above completed, land's surface wind searches.
Asters and thistles, dark stalks with golden grass perches.
Red cedar bristles, purple fruits in the foliage,
the waxy cones sealed against winter's harsh spoilage.

Wind glides through naked canes of fence-line plum,
rattles dead forbs, puffy seeds poof on the run.
Flowing around cedar, it whips and twists into eddies,
plucking soil bits, sifts debris into wee waves and levies.

Lying flat, tall grass encasing on thatch dried and browned,
face to warm sun, backside on matted, frigid ground.
Screened from the exploring breath just a few feet distant,
senses contract to focus on the immediate instant.

Warmth seeps down into clothing, pink light on closed eyes.
Cold creeps up to saturate back, butt, and thighs.
Vision up a floral chimney, narrow with vast distance,
hearing sharpens to wind's clash against plants' resistance.

The mind views life's layers, many now just trivial,
pursuing existence beyond creeds so parochial.
It must exceed the physical – wind's endless investigation,
revealing earth's bedrock with irresistible excavation.

For even though deviating from its primal appointment,
tempted here, disturbed there, distorting in airy deportment,
there is a magnetism subtle but compelling,
sparking the intention to uncover ancient dwellings.

Is not our essence kindred to the restless air,
our blusters and vanity just mistakes to repair?
Volatile urgings of contrition move thoughts to dig deep,
making peace and harmony a prize to obtain and keep.

INDIAN SUMMER TWILIGHT

VENERABLE PASSAGE

With the expiring green tanning
comes a bridge of time appearing
between summer and winter spanning
when nature's spirit is whispering.

Bathed in welcome gold, cold sunshine
the dancing wind shakes and shifts.
Indian summer's midnight rhyme,
into slumber the flora drifts.

Therein, gracefulness is instilled.
A temporary beauty distilled.
Painted as mellow vivifications
forming faint tints of rubifications,
rust, citron, and silver exclamations.

The weathering final remnants,
proud shadows of past vitality,
dispersing the future descendants,
defying the law of finality –
binding ancients to immortality.

OPTIMISM

Few moments, when spirits restore,
as when sunlight showers the land
between cloud's fingered hand
during a drab, dark, dreary chore.

Let the next wave of cold creep
with its bleak, wet, soaking shivering.
For holes in the clouds will again be slivering
and warmth will into us surely seep.

CARRY IN THOUGHT

However many cliffs or rifts,
disorienting turns and twists
in your journey of life,
may there, in fond thought, always be
kindred spirits for memory
to bridge the widest strife.

ULTIMATE EXCURSION

Shirt of flannel when I go,
durable jeans from waist to toe.
Hiking boots that fit just right,
baseball cap to shade my sight.
Put a strong stick in my hand,
off to explore the Milky Way land.

With hundred billion shiny stars,
must be crusty planet just like ours.
Looking for one lush, green and blue
with life evolving and creatures new.
But each Pangea will be unique
fitting the orb's chemical physique.

Don't need to see entire universe,
this galaxy enough to traverse.
Starting with trip to very center,
will crawl to rim but dare not enter.
Find what powers gravity's crushing pull
by peering down funnel's mystic black hole.

Dodging through planetary nebulae,
brilliant ultraviolet light on display.
Stellar winds driving celestial soot,
supernova with whirling pulsar root.
Then out to Milky Way's swirling arms
with fields of new stars and planet farms.

Set up a suitable resting place
on piece of debris at edge of space.
Let the disk rotate past, wide but thin,
two hundred million years for one spin.
Plenty of time to make an inspection,
plan one year for each star's collection.

Endless adventure for eternity
as we witness Wisdom's creativity.
Grab your favorite hiking attire,
come join the quest after you retire.
We'll again be children running free
in a playground of diversity.

TRUST

Time took everything from me.
Well, everything, that is,
which always came easy and free.
In return, what turned to be
for pain and weak memory,
stumbling to pay the fee,
is a prize only long life can earn
by mistakes and trying to learn –
Trust! Trust that God will not be stern.

WINTER'S REPOSE

NURTURING

The dark sky frees the icy flake,
sailing silky, the ground to cake.
Lightly landing so as not to disturb
while erasing from sight the summer's herb.

A soothing blanket, silently forming,
it deeply layers 'til spring comes warming.
White and graceful, the fabric of purity
quilting maternal roots with security.

Now cold to flow and freezing wind to blow,
but no concern to dormant life below.
The land snuggled from toe to breast,
a time to heal, a time to rest.

SYLVAN SHRINE

Old road abandoned, used by very few,
just those seeking absence of prying eyes.
Saplings, brambles, grasses, and weeds renew,
reclaiming what was first their proper prize.

Vegetative tunnel pressing in from fenced field,
no sun, billowing clouds hang suspended.
Old woods at distant end, its entrance now concealed,
neglected for decades, its needs soon attended.

Afternoon late, shortest day about to cease,
a dusky world, grayer with each pace.
Light at horizon, cloud's belly lit in its crease,
rich scarlet red, with purple west face.

Radiance rises, then subsides to brief orange glow,
leaving a place darker prior to the escaping light.
Loneliness seeps at dusk, soaking in at twilight's flow,
determination in the morning; truth in the dark night.

Within the exalted tree's candle-dim cathedral
shadowy trunks rise into umbrella spread.
Obstinate leaves dangle dry to rattle orchestral,
the stately sentinels follow my foreign tread.

Silently, suddenly, wet snow starts to sail
large, heavy, and thick. Brushing a ghostly mark,
highlighting white the worn coon runs and deer trail,
pasting the wind face in each tree's furrowed bark.

The wet leaves draw silent, melting into snow's swish.
No other sound, no movement of life far or near,
just a sanctuary of sylvan mix with the wish
that I was not walking among them here.

At this moment, so primal and surreal,
humble reverence for the hallowed arboreal.

SIMPLE SUBSISTENCE

Miles high, within frigid clouds of mist,
fine, dusty particles and moisture mix.
Icy molecules bond, crystals fix,
in updrafts growing, snowflakes persist
until gravity they can't resist.

From West across to Mississippi;
"On your way?" meadow vole does ask,
"Give a shelter, an easy task.
Cover the land with your silent sea.
Delay and do this bit for me."

Swirling, whirling flakes of snow,
delicate crystals starry finned,
sideways slanting, kiting the wind.
Skittering, sliding to old fence row,
filling the swales with blustery blow.

Burying deep in crusty white
the withered grass and plant debris,
roofing the straw, setting the vole free
to roam its world beneath all sight
in hazy aurora of filtered light.

From a bed of soft milkweed fluff,
now safe from wind, fox, and raptor,
scoots on trails crisscrossing the pasture
fetching fall's bounty stored in the duff,
seeds of weeds, shrubs, and dried, tasty stuff.

With nest, larder, and security,
lives a tranquil life, very quiet and meek.
What it doesn't need, it doesn't seek.
Partaking from nature's charity,
contentment springs from obscurity.

SOLE ENCOUNTER

Stirred to action, travel to initiate,
what purpose that harsh forces can't placate?
A hop and a spring lifts into the air,
solitary movement, not as a pair.
Exposed, yet undaunted, the flight to begin,
determined, the goal known only to him.
North, into cold's frigid space,
raw into wind's bitter face.

Over the dirty snow and cloddy tillage,
no interest in carcass or grain to pillage.
Without temptation to shelter where creek trees grow,
no calling or cawing, just shadow does it throw.
Strength powers ebony wings' choppy beat,
distance the apparent reward to reap.
Arrow straight, intent on its single quest,
too soon beyond sight over hill's far crest.

No return, no revisit, gone to last,
our one brief encounter now is past.
What history molds this enigmatic bird,
what secrets has the nomadic creature heard?
Which one stands at fatiguing flight's expiration –
a committed duty or chance for preservation?
Do past sins demand such compensation
to reach a pure cove for reconciliation?

Are triumphs and sorrows in yesterday,
how many companions drifted away?
Was it defeated, now dashing to escape,
or a pleasure does it now anticipate?
This feathered fowl dressed as in inky sorrow,
do good friends and times await its tomorrow?
Behind its ruby eyes, only its mind does know –
how many mortals think like this crow?

RADIANCE

Across the sifting white plateau
frosting swirls texture the swells.
Silence the loudest sound that wells
over the deeply bedded snow.
The heavens canvass the frozen pearl
with rich colors, while the art grows
rising into a lofty mural.
First silver, then flaming orange flows,
dyed brightly as day's last light goes.

Entrancing are the painted skies
performing beyond earth's crest
as evening comes to rest.
The sun has dipped below the eyes,
a wavy cirrus cloud softly lies
with bold brush strokes across the west.
So intense, only nature can comprise,
glowing with red and scarlet's best.

An effervescent panorama rolled,
unable to touch, ever so distant,
constantly changing with every instant.
Can't possess to be bought or sold,
a precious sight here in the cold.

No words record the feelings that fold
into moments of pure detachment
from the world's laborious enactment.
Wish to save in a jar or by mold
to enjoy each nightfall as I grow old.

The distant atmosphere absorbs the blue
and long, red wavelengths produce the hue
shining from the cloud's icy under.
It's all part of life's mystical wonder –
music, colors and dreams in slumber.
What other starry orb displays as much,
and why do we recognize beauty as such?

With the vanished sun's inspiring glow,
such majesty to see here below!
Blessed was I to witness the light leap,
how fitting such splendor before sleep.
It renews the deep spiritual notion
that time extends past one life's motion.
Spirit blends with nature to become whole,
even more glories await the free soul.

THE HIKER'S PRAYER

Judge me harshly for yesterday
if I have not improved my way.
Where dark trespasses were planned
and regret shows not its hand,
a mean trek without consideration,
mark this sad soul for condemnation.

Mock me for a false forgiveness
while hiking blind to own weakness.
My life's track a twisted, winding affair
yet denounce others with pompous air.
Then bring to fair trial the hypocrisy,
chastise the lack of kind democracy.

But judge leniently my daily fray
if past transgressions do heavily weigh.
Where missed steps draw free admission
and from harm blooms just contrition.
Then as night's vain mist burns away
let my journey yield truth each day.

ABOUT ATMOSPHERE PRESS

Founded in 2015, Atmosphere Press was built on the principles of Honesty, Transparency, Professionalism, Kindness, and Making Your Book Awesome. As an ethical and author-friendly hybrid press, we stay true to that founding mission today.

If you're a reader, enter our giveaway for a free book here:

SCAN TO ENTER
BOOK GIVEAWAY

If you're a writer, submit your manuscript for consideration here:

SCAN TO SUBMIT
MANUSCRIPT

And always feel free to visit Atmosphere Press and our authors online at atmospherepress.com. See you there soon!

ABOUT THE AUTHOR

Born and raised in Iowa, **BILL HAYWOOD** spent 10 years managing prairies and woodlands for Black Hawk County Conservation Board. He then started Forest Improvement Services and spent nearly 30 years renewing degraded woodlands on private land across Iowa. Following retirement, he embraced two hobbies: making unique tables and benches from slabs cut out of discarded tree trunk sections and writing poetry. While hand-finishing the wood pieces, writing provided a mental diversion and an opportunity to share his lifelong outdoor experiences and appreciation of the natural world.

Bill and his wife, Wahneta, raised six daughters and continue to live on their small acreage near Janesville, Iowa.